Minivan Poems

Justin Grimbol

What follows is some legally binding and serious shit:

THICKE & VANEY PRESS

www.thickeandvaney.com

ISBN: 978-0-9981504-1-3

LCCN: 2016955995

T&V№ 1516

Copyright © Justin Grimbol

Cover Art by Jon Kalish

Editted by Thomas Vanesworthy III

All rights reserved. No part of this book may be reproduced or transmitted in any form, including semaphore signals, or by any means, electronic or mechanical or angelic, in-cluding photocopying, recording, tattoos, or by any information storage and retrieval system, without the written consent of the publisher, except where permitted by law, even during a zombie apocalypse.

This is a work of fiction. Names, characters, pales, and incidents are either products of the author's imagination or are used fictitiously, and any resemblance to actual events or persons, living, dead, or undead, is entirely coincidental.

Printed in the United States of America. God save the Queen.

For Seb Doubinsky

My Minivan prays
For its brakes
To give out

My Minivan will stare at your legs
My Minivan will stare at your butt
My Minivan will stare at your elbows
My Minivan will stare at the gum
On your shoe

My Minivan is addicted to the communion wine

Which is nothing more than grape juice

My Minivan is a ghost hunter

Driving through small towns

Seeing a home with lights on at

Three in the morning

Imagining comfort

My Minivan will sniff your ass

My Minivan will get fat off yellow lines

My Minivan will remember

A silence Minivans were never meant

To remember

My Minivan has the sweetest eyes
And the wiggliest butt
My Minivan
Is happy to see me

My Minivan is very open minded when it
Comes to fucking around with other Minivans

Minivan
No Like
Yoga

My Minivan does not do the dishes
My Minivan uses paper plates

My Minivan hates the holidays and
My Minivan hates vacations
My Minivan wants to drive around
My Minivan wants to look for stuff

My Minivan tried to be a Buddhist

It tried meditation once

But it couldn't sit still, because it's

A Minivan

For

Fuck's sake

My Minivan believes in second hand smoke

My Minivan believes in the way

Your lap smells so well

My Minivan breaks laws
My Minivan
Doesn't even have
Seat belts

My Minivan is filthy
And filled with empty
Soda cans

Go ask my Minivan questions
My Minivan only gives bad advice
It's better that way
Trust me

My Minivan finds creeks

And ghost-colored skies that look

Like the world is either ending

Or beginning

My Minivan will ruin any diet
My Minivan will never turn
Into a car

My Minivan can
Dance with your
Butt

Read all the dead bugs
On my Minivan's hood
My Minivan has killed and my Minivan
Will kill again

My Minivan finds a rundown

Diner and orders

A grilled cheese sandwich

My Minivan has no back seats
There is a mattress back there
With just enough room for me to sleep
Comfortably
But...
My Minivan
Rarely lets me
Sleep alone

My Minivan

Stares at the missing steeple
Of my mother's church
She is dead now and my Minivan's
High beams look for her darkness

My Minivan has a heart

And that heart

Smells like sweaty armpits

And of

Women who were hippy mechanics of laughter

And eye rolling

My Minivan doubles its grief every trip

Because my Minivan loves you so much.

My Minivan

Knows the morning light is warm

And heavy as laughter

My Minivan
Empties me
Into lonely towns

There are church pews in this Minivan
And they are hard and
Thank your butt with hardness

There are tumbleweeds disguised
As people out there and there are
Rivers disguised puddles

The ferry

Carries my Minivan

To wherever it wants to go

And

Some days

The waves

Get swollen

And

The boat

Feels like it will tip over

Or

It's trying to

Pray

My Minivan has found
Sniffable mountains

My Minivan

Drives out onto the salt flats

Licking the ground

Tasting

The sweat

Of the sun

My Minivan cuddles

With the sea lions in Astoria

My Minivan

Uses the shadows

Of redwoods

As lingerie

My Minivan

Shops in Beverly Hills

My Minivan will turn this church into a parking garage

My Minivan will argue
Until we are both lightheaded

My

Minivan

Will drive

The highways

Until it's cracked

And curved

And forgotten

My Minivan finds neglect

To be a sacred thing

My Minivan has three hearts
One in its headlights
One in its radio
One in its ass
Growing larger
And more touchable
With each
Memory

Listen with all your grief

There will be Minivans

There will be the glowing asses

Of the fireflies

Above the field

Let my Minivan be
Dog tongued

Pray to the prayer

My Minivan has great ideas

My Minivan's

Soul

Feels

Like

A

Wedgie

My Minivan is filled with old people

And they all

Have to

Pee

My Minivan
Has soft hands
From
Minivanning
Too long

My Minivan doesn't dream about prison
Or going to high school as a naked thirty
year old man

My
Minivan has dungeons
That will both hide me from the snow
And take me into it

My Minivan watches the stars to make sure
They don't steal stuff

My Minivan

Gets drunk

And wakes up roadless

And sweet

And lovable

My Minivan scratches the road like a lottery ticket
My
Minivan wins itself broke

My Minivan

Remembers how Minivans

Were meant to live

My Minivan wants to know where old men drink their coffee
My Minivan wants to go
Places that stay put like moles and bad knees and stray dogs

My
Minivan
Prays to
The
Diner Gods

My Minivan

Listens To

Only

The

Greasiest

Gossip

My Minivan loves inside jokes
Which means my Minivan loves
Poetry

I talk too much

And

Now my Minivan

Knows all my codes

Which are even better

Than secrets

My Minivan loves
Empty homes

My Minivan

Has opinions

My Minivans

Heart smells

Like a butt

The best sunset

Is a porch light

This is whiskey

To my Minivan

My Minivan
Wonders if it's hunting season
My Minivan thinks everything
Sounds like a gun

My Minivan

Looks up the skirt

Of the desert

My Minivan
Hikes up
Vermont's
Tallest sledding hills

My Minivan loves your truck nuts

My Minivan is secure in its sexuality

My Minivan will do stuff

My Minivan
Bungee jumps
Into
Romance

My Minivan

Needs

Adult-sized diapers

Whenever

It looks

Into your eyes

My Minivan

Moves in and makes

Itself goddamned comfortable

My Minivan smokes all your weed

My Minivan has long, impossible legs
That cause anxiety
So
Don't climb these legs
Don't dangle from the pubes
Be safe
Avoid Minivan
The road says heroic things
As it curves with the river
It passes by old farms
And farmers who
Sit on their porch
Reading Clive Cussler

All weather belongs to my Minivan
Even the raunchy kind
My Minivan has a history of picnics

My Minivan will sing hymns badly
With old ladies
Loaded with remorse
And the tide

My Minivan will laugh the past away

Then drive to it

My Minivan will drive past hills

Covered in golden rod

My Minivan is empty and love goes on
Like tall grass bent by the wind
My Minivan chases its own tail
And swims the road naked

My Minivan has been fired as a Minivan

Many times

But it keeps working as a Minivan

Regardless

My Minivan

Sheds lottery tickets

My Minivan listens to audio books

Of stories children have written

In magic marker

Spelling

Every word wrong and better

My Minivan knows of church basements

Filled with

Wood paneling and coffee in Styrofoam cups

And

People playing spin the bottle

Not really knowing how the game works

Anymore

The bottle

That poor lonely bottle

Just keeps spinning

Baby

My Minivan borrows
A lot of money from my dad

My Minivan

Doesn't like coffee

My Minivan

Drives better

When it's tired

My Minivan knows what sleep feels like

Sleep

With

Butts

Is its

True north

My Minivan

Hears sexy saxophones

In old bridges

Collapsed farms

The rumps of fireflies

Dirt roads

And closed up store fronts

My Minivan

Throws its prayers

Into every river it drives over

My Minivan

Goes fishing

Just by driving by

The lake

And knowing

The fish are there

My Minivan has

Fog brain

And

It doesn't

Want

A cure

My Minivan is only enlightened

When it feels stupid

My Minivan

Is pregnant

With a little

Abandoned

Church

In

Its belly

My Minivan
Burps
Sound
Like
Church
Bells

Blood is thicker than water
But blood is not
Thicker
Than Minivan

My Minivan worries

About meditation

And boredom

And inner something

Too often

Instead of just

Driving around

And stuff

My Minivan does not watch

Porn

But

My

Mini

Van

Will stalk you

On Facebook

My Minivan is a fucking Minivan
Even when it is being pulled by a horse

My Minivan is a tent sometimes
And I sleep in the back
On the single mattress
With my wife
And my dog
And the cold air

My Minivan

Will expose itself

And nothing will be in there to see it

But me

My Minivan has so many anxiety issues

It has like thirty eight anxiety issues

Maybe more

Maybe like thirty nine anxiety issues

Cavemen

Used to ride Minivans

And fight with their cave spouses

And go on road trips

Before there were roads

My Minivan

Feels lonely

And lost

But only

When I

Am

Inside

It

My Minivan trains hard
Everyday so it can be lazy

And stoned

And still move

And sweat

And want

To be with

Everything

My Minivan

Is obviously going

To summer camp

My Minivan

Wouldn't miss that

For anything in the world

My mini

Van

Will visit

Your family

This holiday season

And talk to your dad about politics

Until things are so tense

Everybody just

Starts to pass out

My Minivan
Fondles its own
Headlights

My Minivan

Doesn't like

Being unfriended

But my

Minivan

Will

Do plenty

Of unfriendly

Things

My Minivan

Appreciates

It's empty

Seats

My Minivan has roots
But they are electric
And stretch out
And move fast
Even when
They are standing
Still

My Minivan drives in and out
Of its own exorcism

My Minivan

Is a haunted house

Or

At least

It smells like one

My Minivan will not be home for the holidays
But it will feel homesick and bedridden for you
My Minivan is tired of traffic sounds
Including its own

My Minivan cuddles so well
My Minivan loves being pregnant

My Minivan doesn't know if the ferry is coming

Or if it can even leave

It waits

Bugs find the headlights

And

Act like it is some sort of family reunion

My Minivan

Sees lights

In the distance

And hopes

It is a pleasant village

And that it

Is really

Really

Far away

And dead

And the light is old

And took a really long

Time to make its way

To my Minivan

My Minivan remembers pizza

It remembers it too often and now it is fat

From all the memories

And

Lovable and can barely fit on the road

My Minivan invented ice

My Minivan

Whimpers

And waits its windows to thaw

My Minivan flirts and gossips

With women in baggy camouflage sweatshirts

My Minivan will flirt with you

In a way that feels motherly

My Minivan is the color of a purple nurple

Which is the color of romance

And

Family

If my Minivan had boobies
They would be
Really firm

My Minivan is not a go-getter

My Minivan knows things

About the sun.

My Minivan sweats dust

And

People draw pictures of penises

In the dust

Then

The

Rain

Comes

The farm houses

The rest stops

The grief-soaked hidden places of its driver

These places feel familiar

My Minivan

Has wanted to fit inside them for so long

My Minivan found its creator

In polar ice caps

Which were melting

Because there were too many

Fucking Minivans in the world

My Minivan has a dick but that doesn't mean

It's male

No way

It's a Minivan

And that's

All

Its own thing

What's my Minivan's advice for healthy looking radiant skin?

POP ALL YOUR ZITS

ASSHOLE

DON'T TAKE TOO MANY BATHS

SNIFF A BUTT

My Minivan
Goes to the gym
And works out
And makes the whole
Gym
Smell like a Minivan

My Minivan

Has had the talk

My Minivan

Has seen birds

And bees

Together

Naked

Not putting it in and doing other stuff too

My Minivan knows when the time is right
My Minivan waits on a hill covered in golden rod
Allergic to the pollen
Sneezing until it looks shiny

My Minivan can't get off the road

The undertow is too strong

My Minivan has lost so many bathing suits

My Minivan is sunburnt

My Minivan hates vacations

Sniff armpits

Stare at butts

Think about butts

While sitting on butts

My Minivan

Will

Loaf hard

Eager for warmth

And always know

It was the snow

Not the sun

That teaches us to slow

Down

And to be warm

My Minivan is

Allergic to cities

My Minivan searches for small

Crusty towns

My Minivan is tired of scratching

Unscratchable things

My Minivan has ghosts

And these ghosts are young

And they are getting younger

They get hurt easily

And I have to protect them

Because

I am their pediatrician

I am their death

My Minivan finds senility in a few things
Every day and that's enough religion
To get me through and full and warm

The dead forget things
That's what they do

My Minivan

Will always feel familiar

The same way

My dog will always smell like the sun

My Minivan has a message for the world
I WANT TWO SLICES OF PIZZA PLEASE
DON'T BOTHER HEATING THEM UP
I ACTUALLY PREFER THEM LUKE WARM

My Minivan

Has trouble finding the end of things

But it will keep trying

With its ass red and its engine coughing

It will find whatever there is to find

Justin Grimbol was raised by Presbyterian ministers in Sag Harbor, New York. He met his wife Heather at Green Mountain College in Vermont. His wife and he move around a lot, but hope to end up back in Vermont one day.

Justin is the author of Drinking Until Morning, The Crud Master (from Eraserhead's New Bizarro Author Series), The Creek, The Party Lords, Hard Bodies, and Naked Friends.

www.ingramcontent.com/pod-product-compliance
Lightning Source LLC
Chambersburg PA
CBHW020618300426
44113CB00007B/699